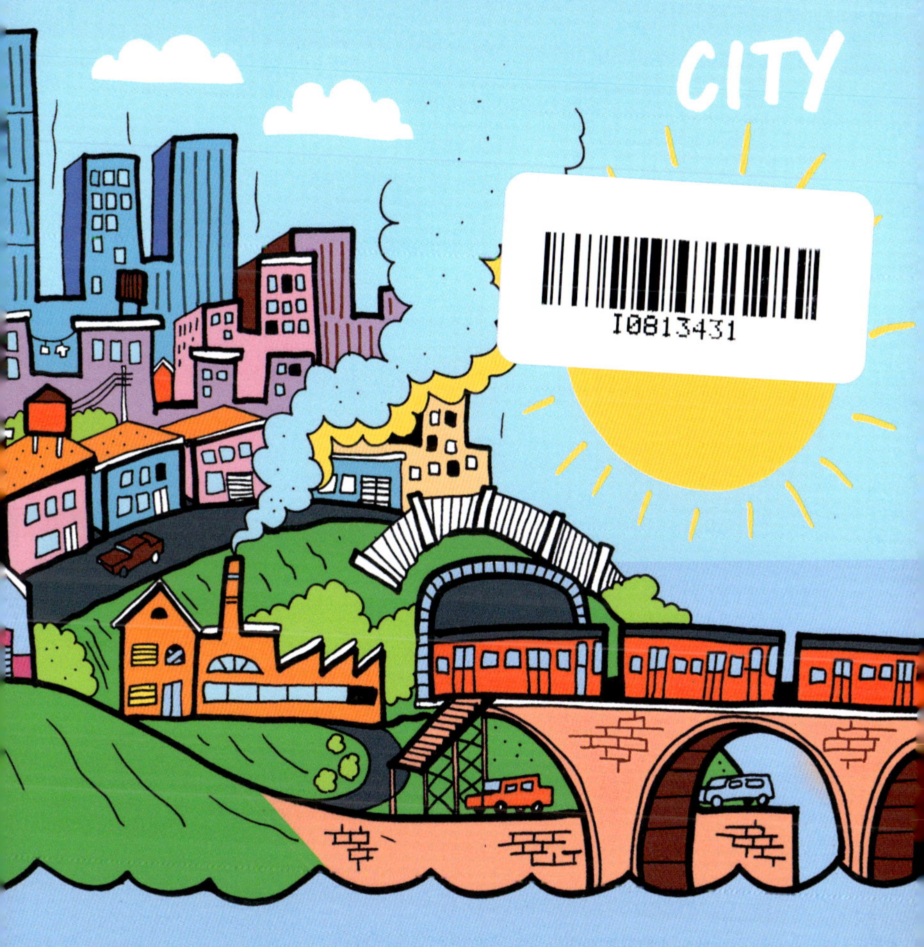
CITY

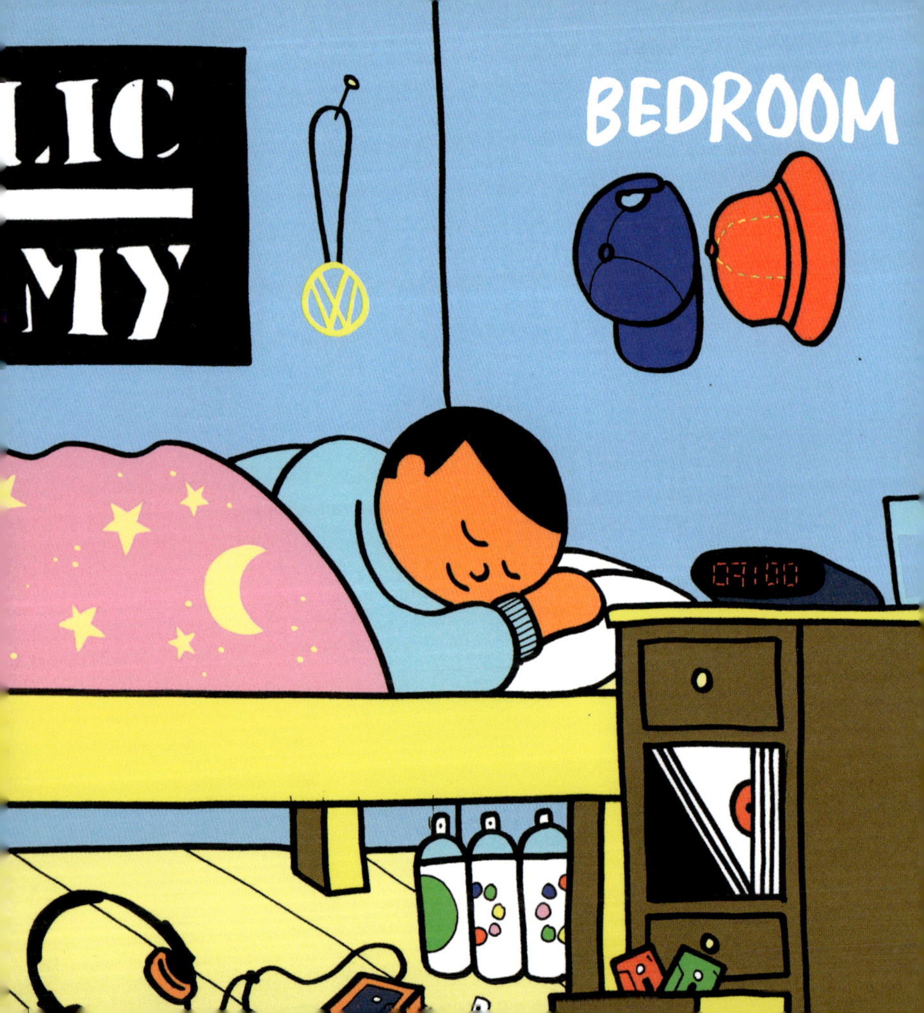
BEDROOM
LIC
MY

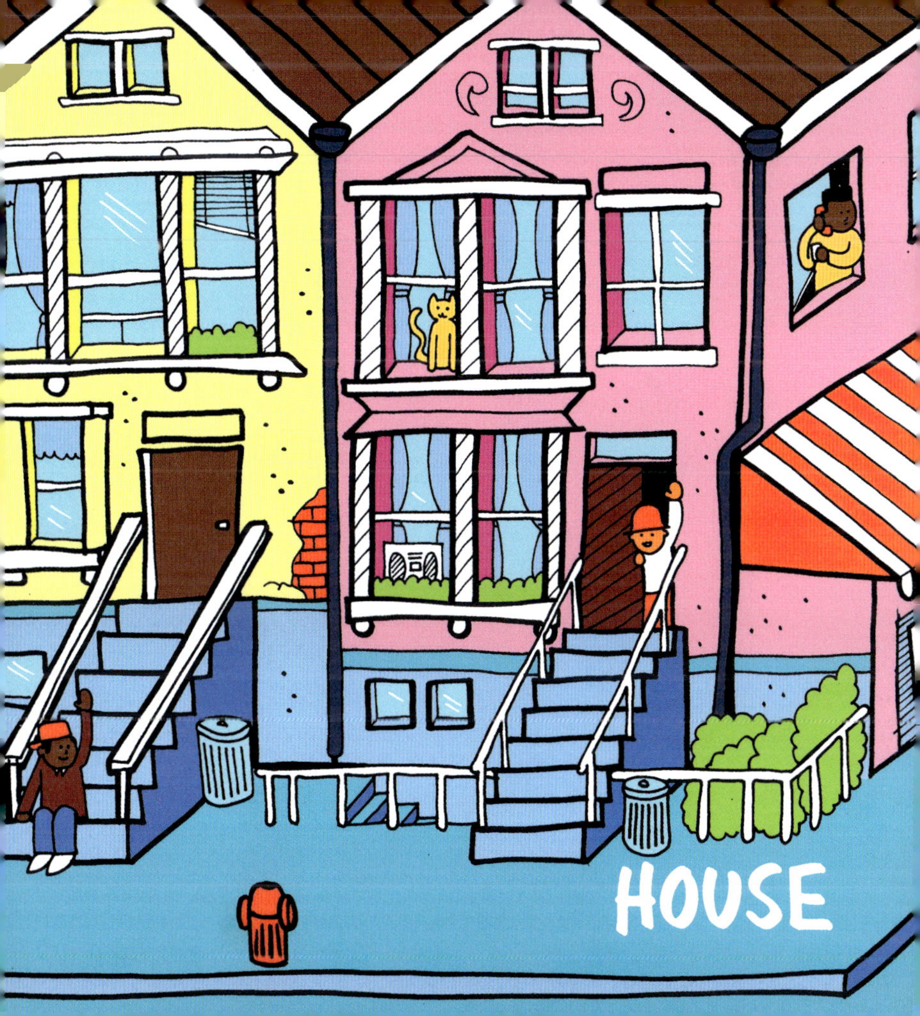
HOUSE

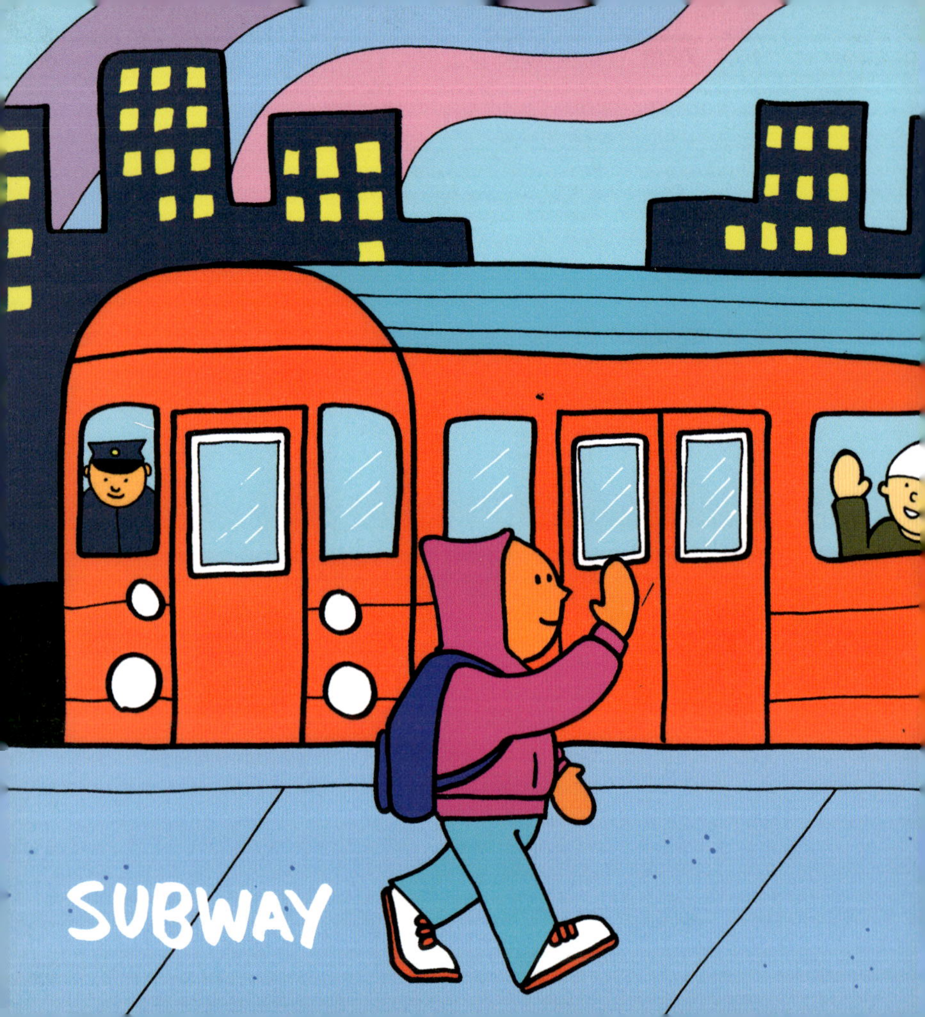
SUBWAY

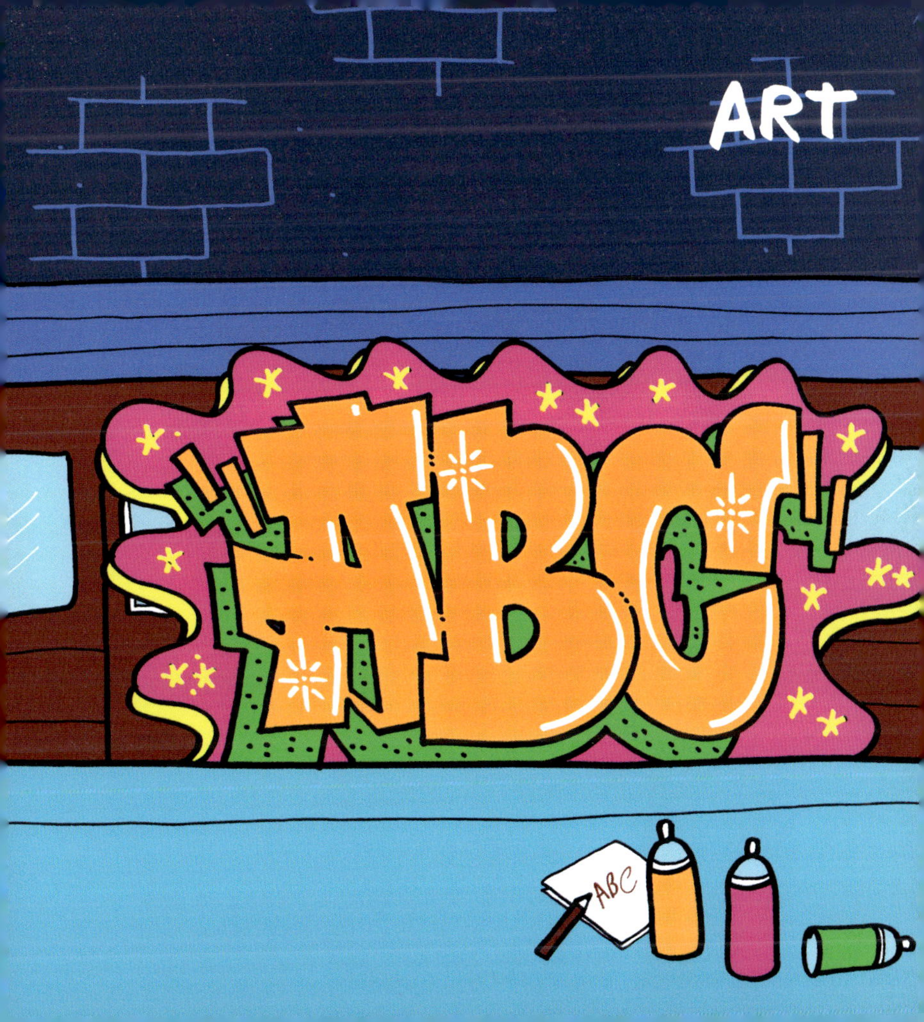

ART

ABC

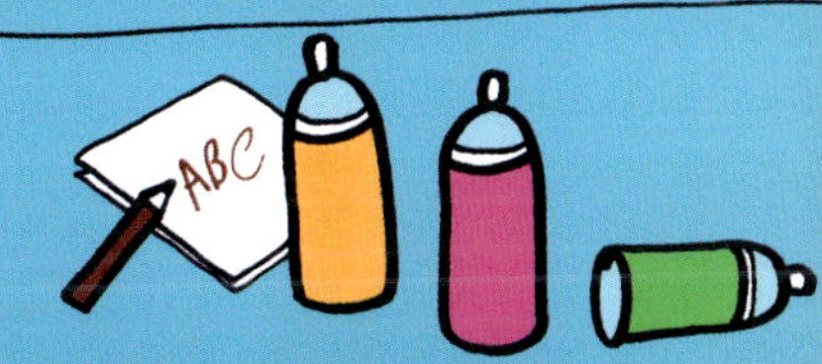

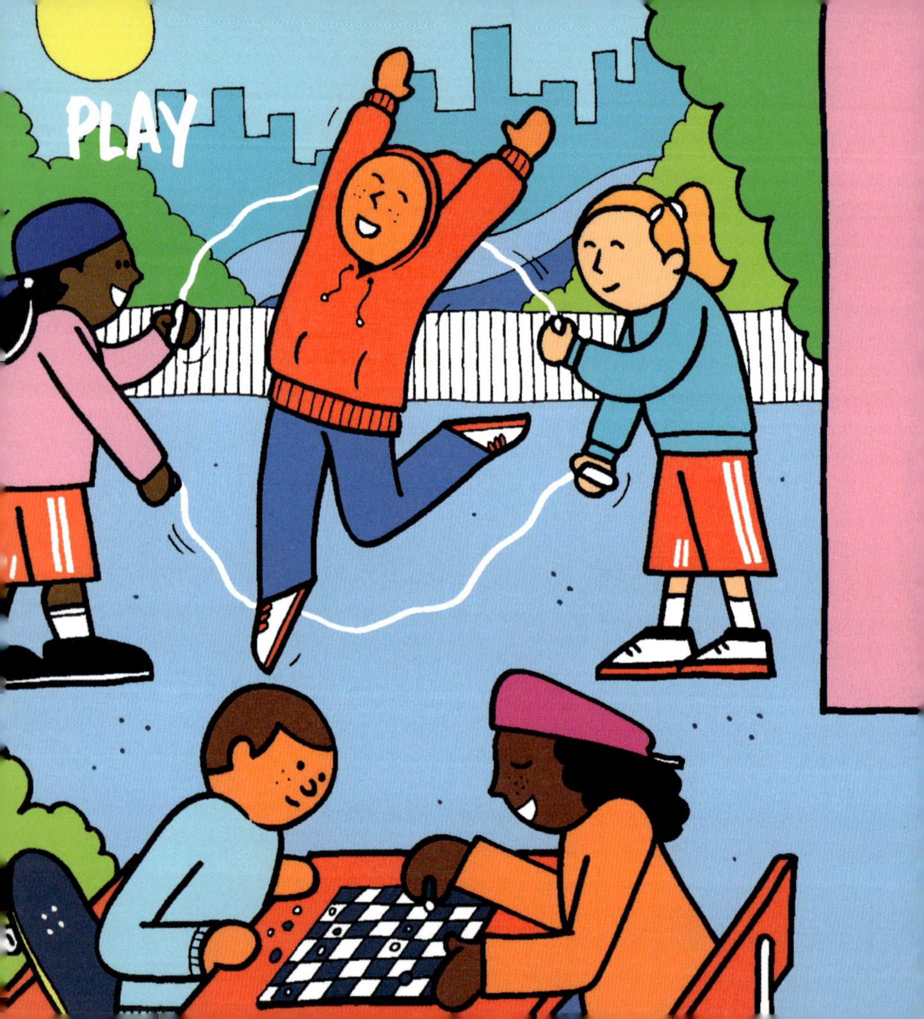
PLAY

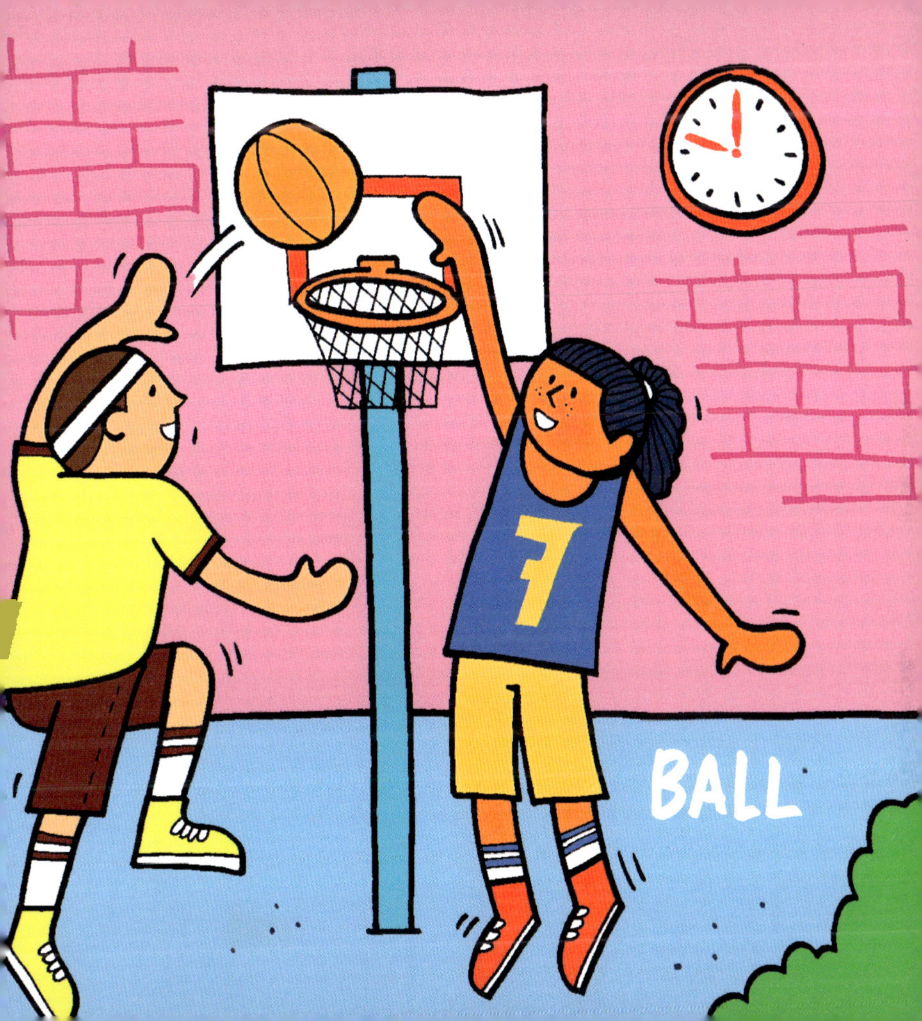
BALL

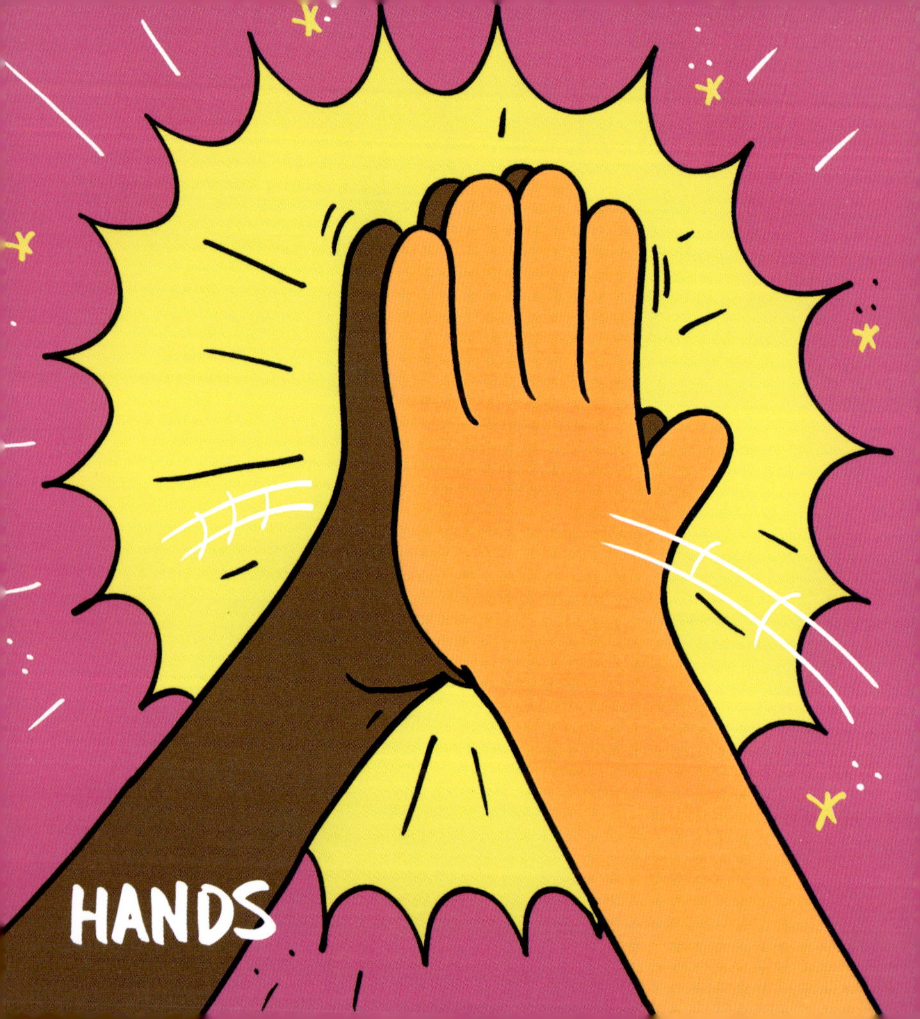
HANDS

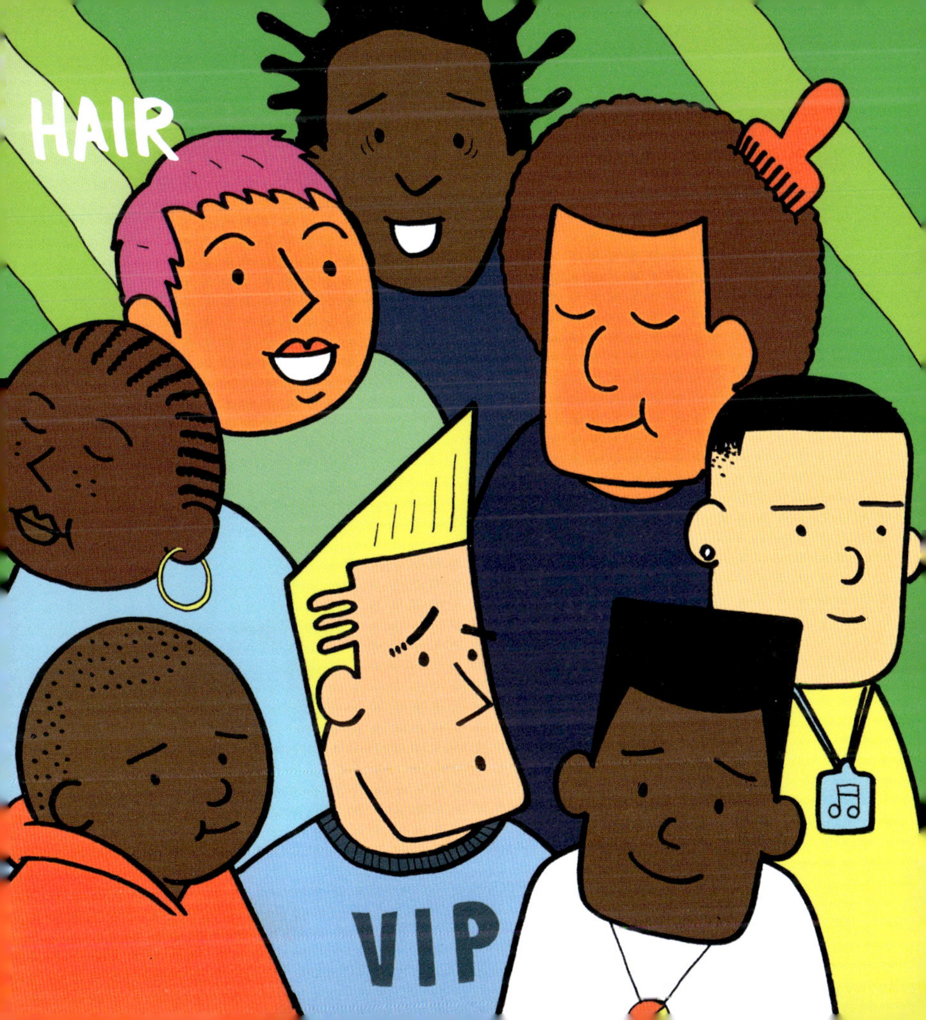
HAIR
VIP

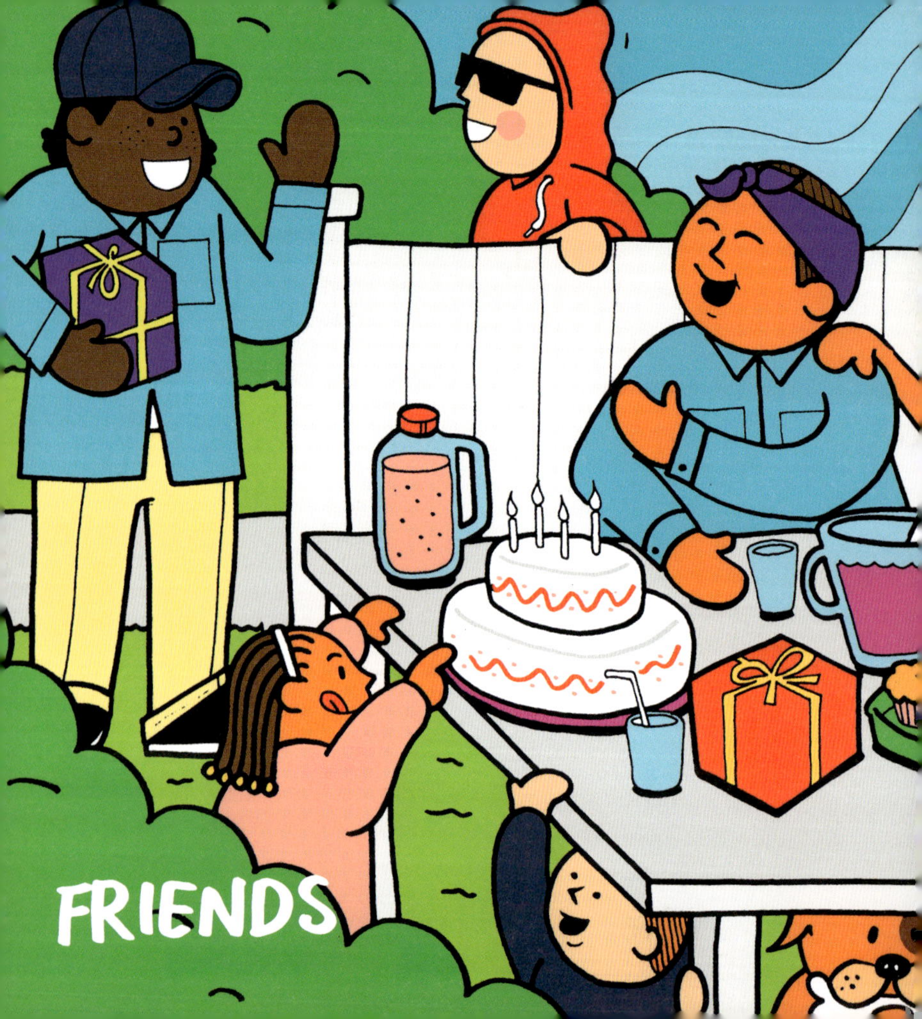
FRIENDS

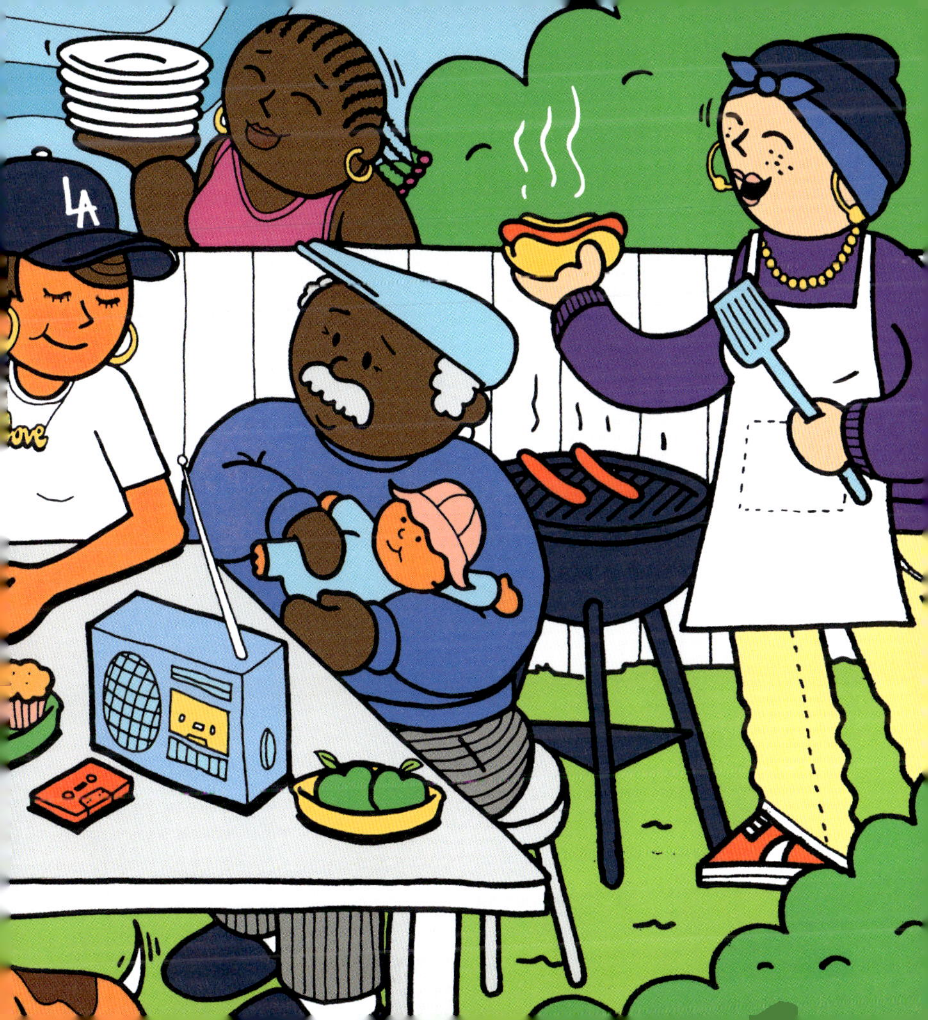
LA

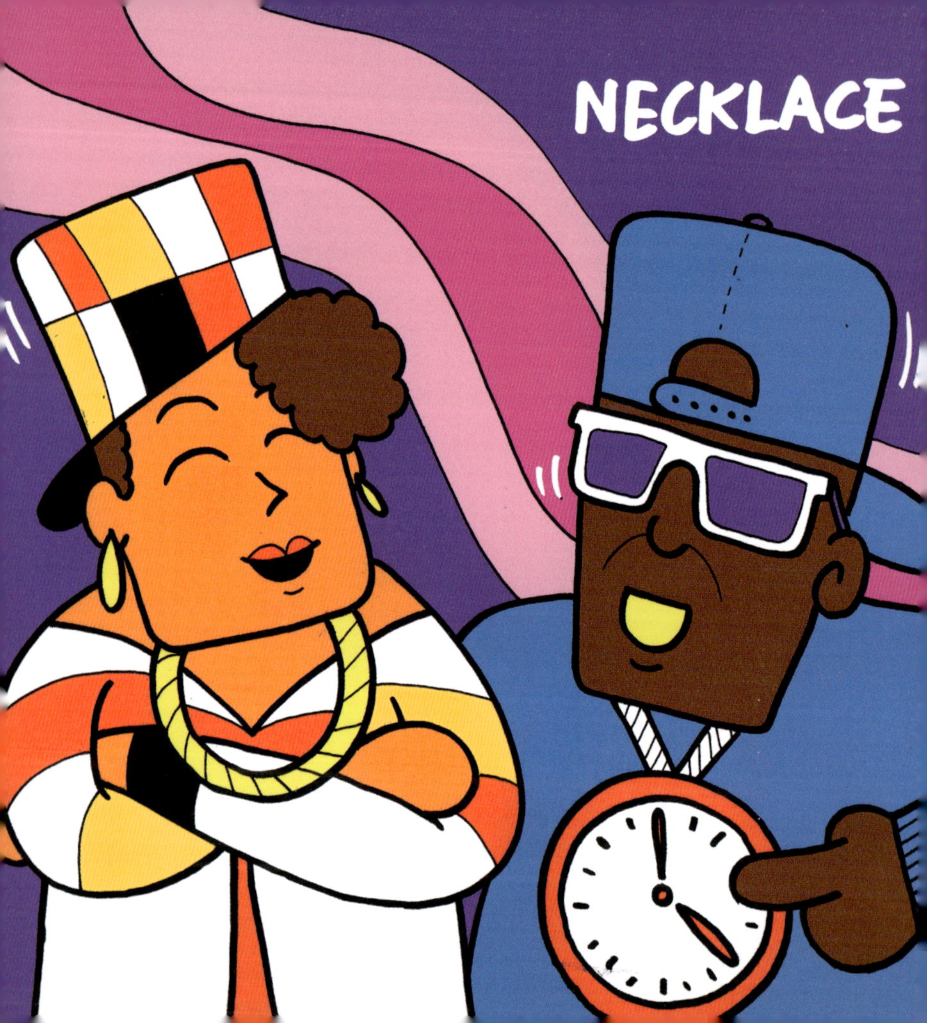
NECKLACE

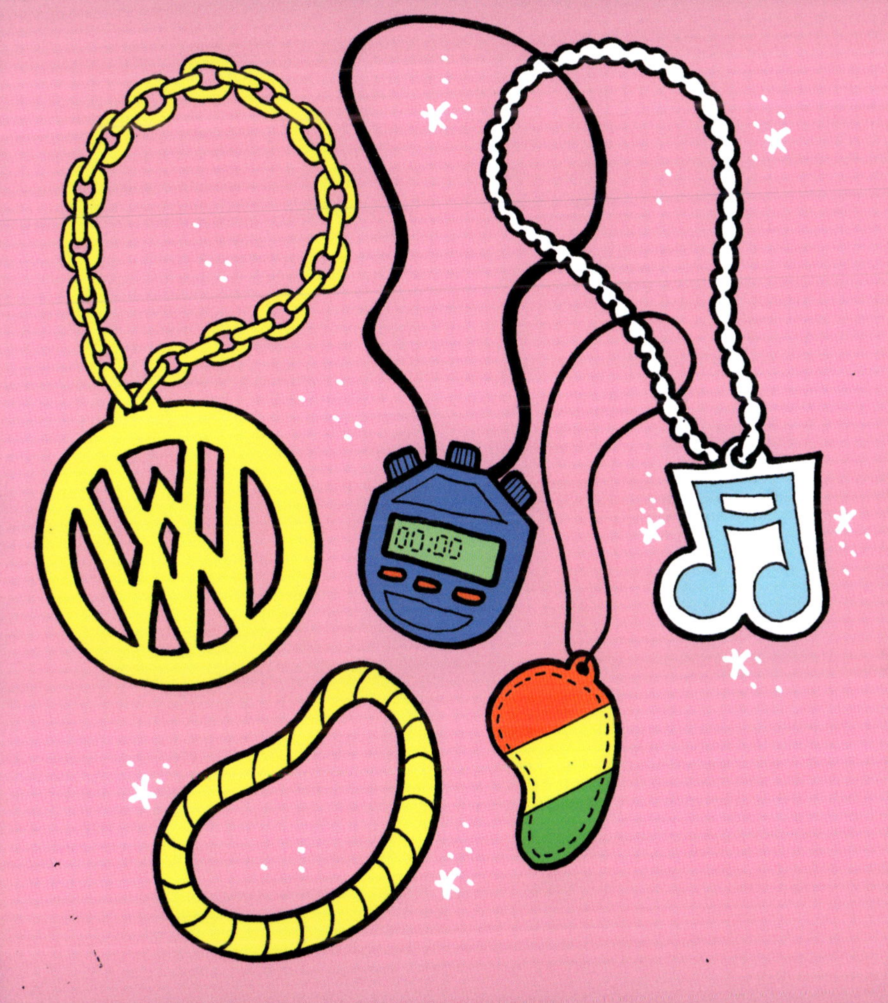
00:00

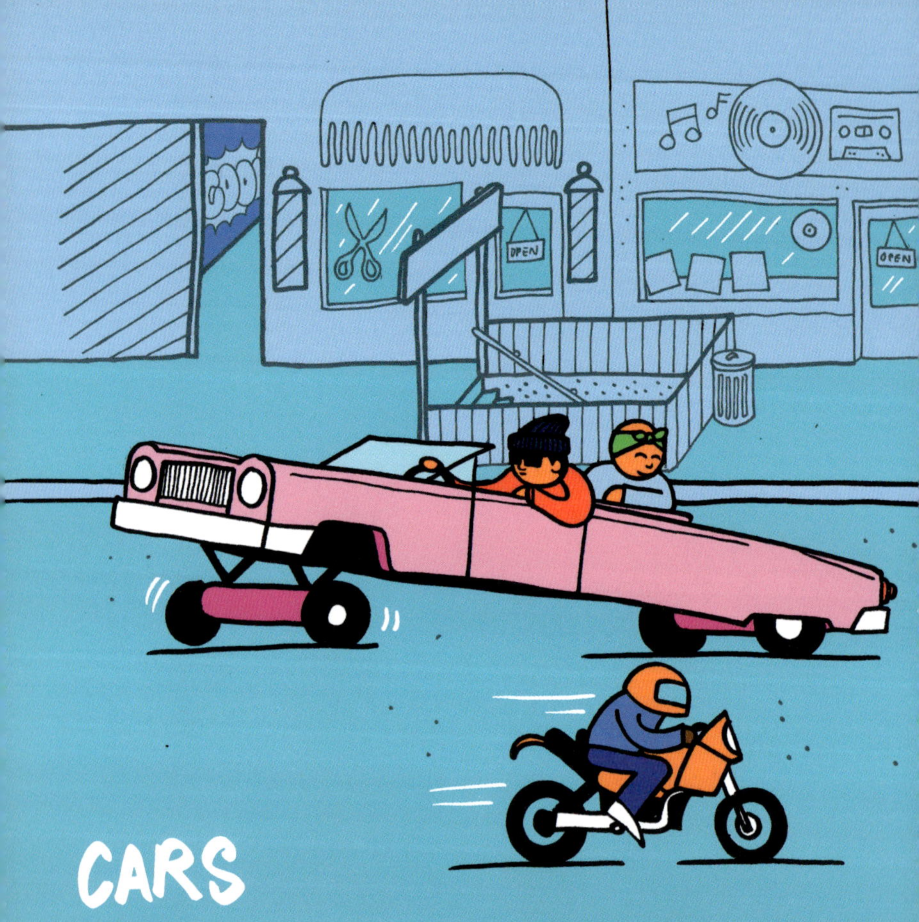

CARS

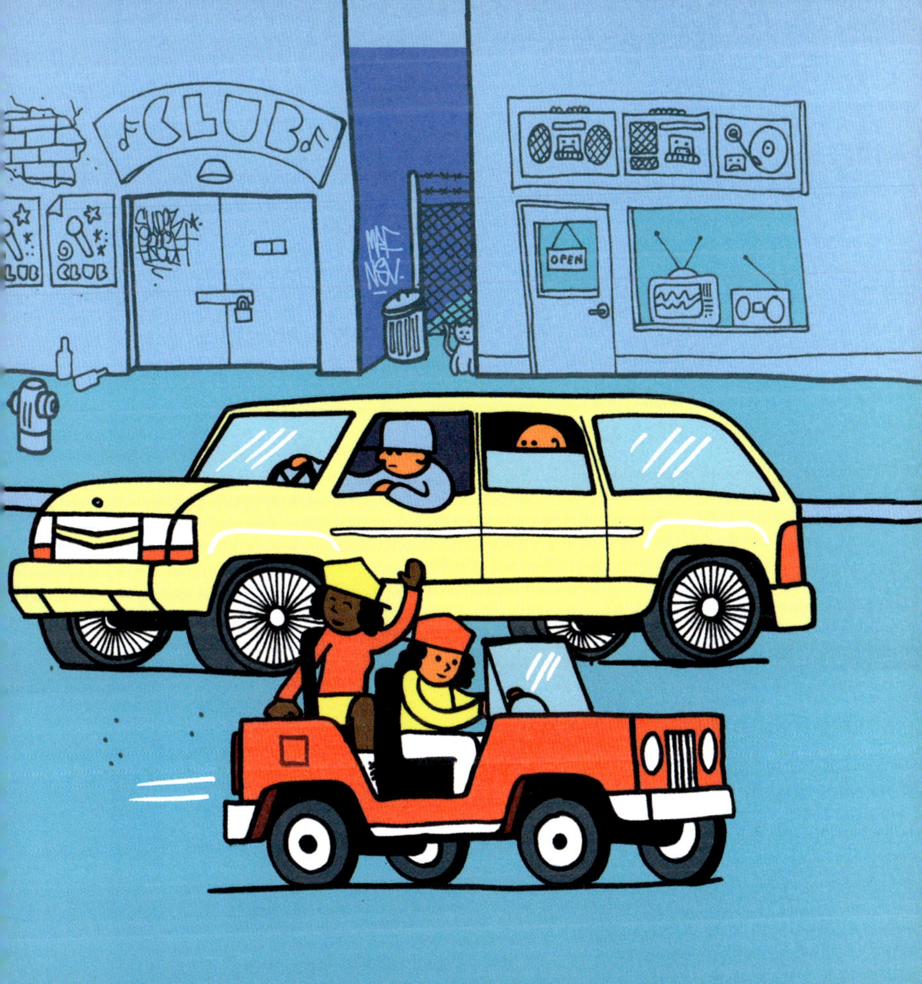

CLUB
CLUB
CLUB
OPEN

HAT

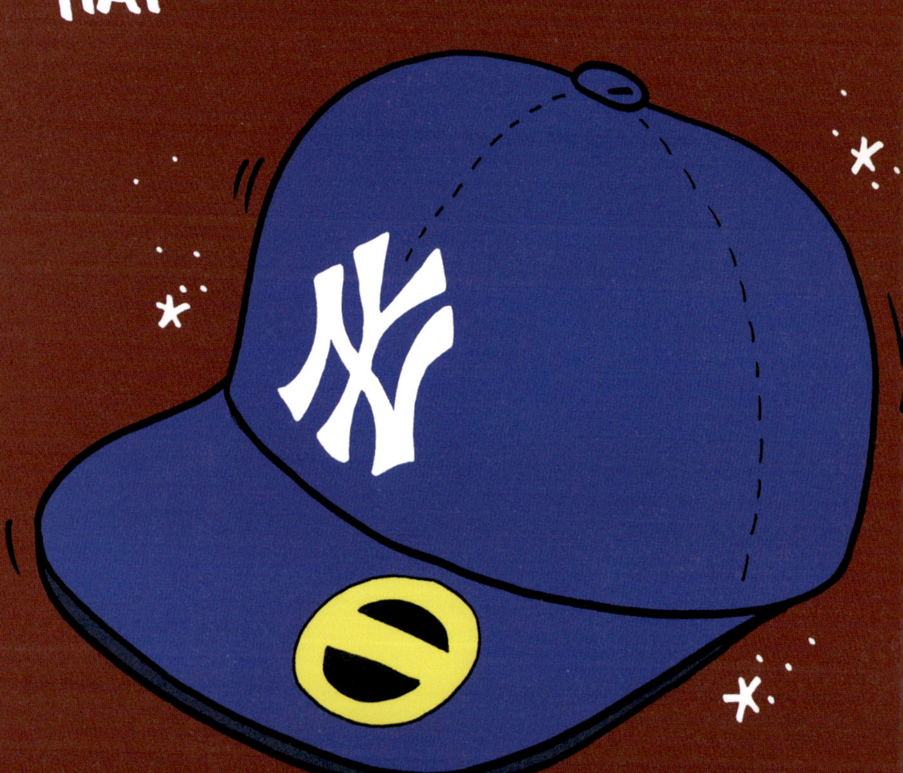

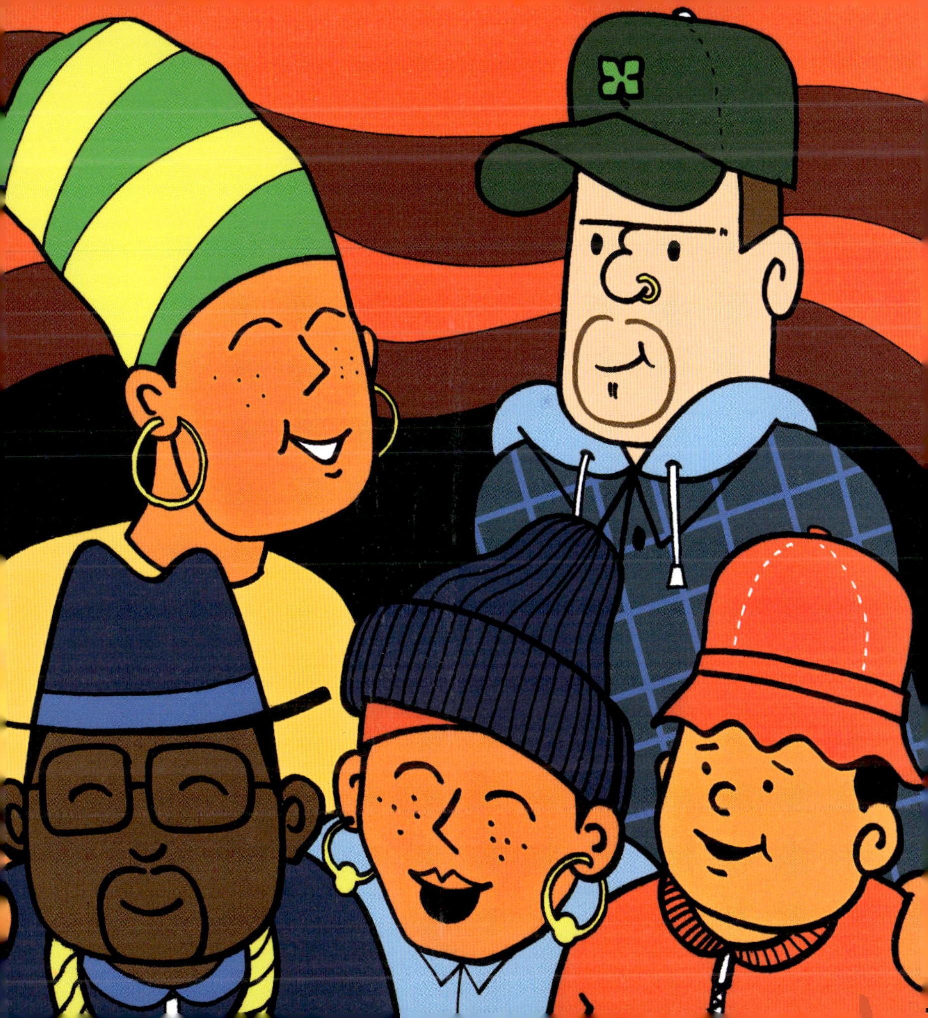

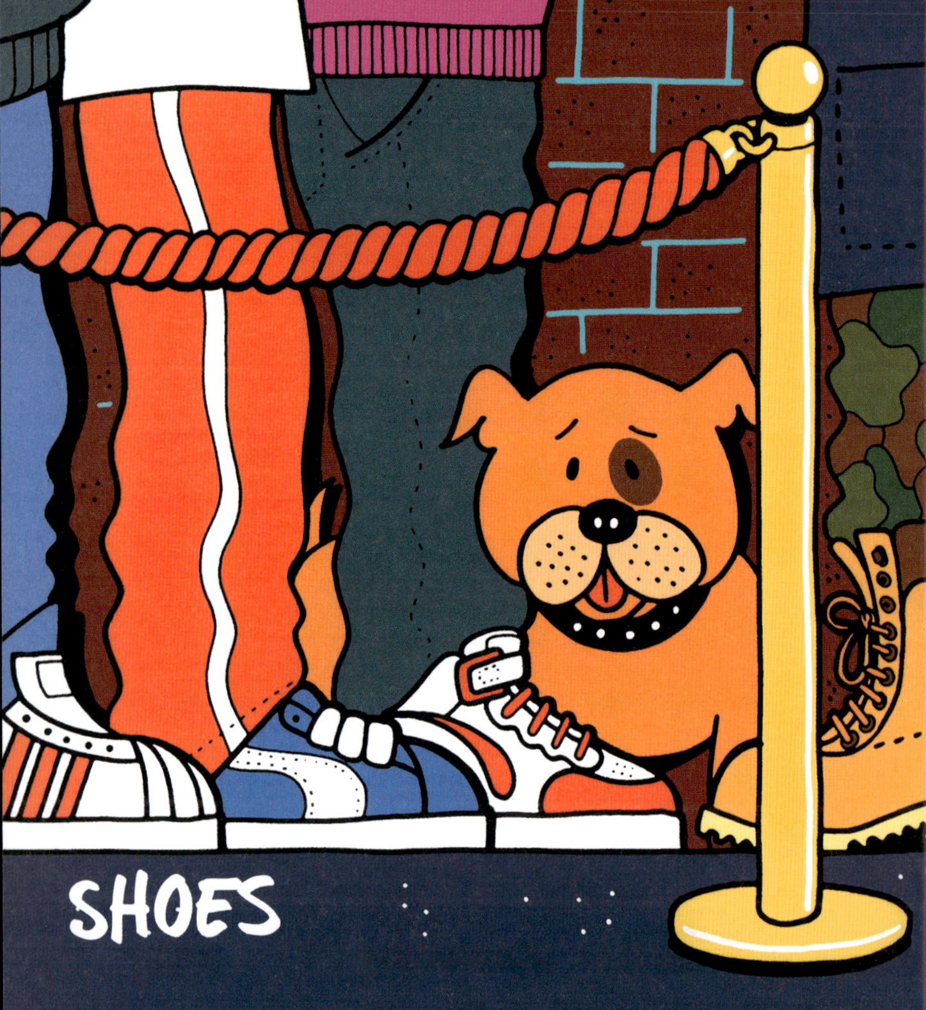
SHOES

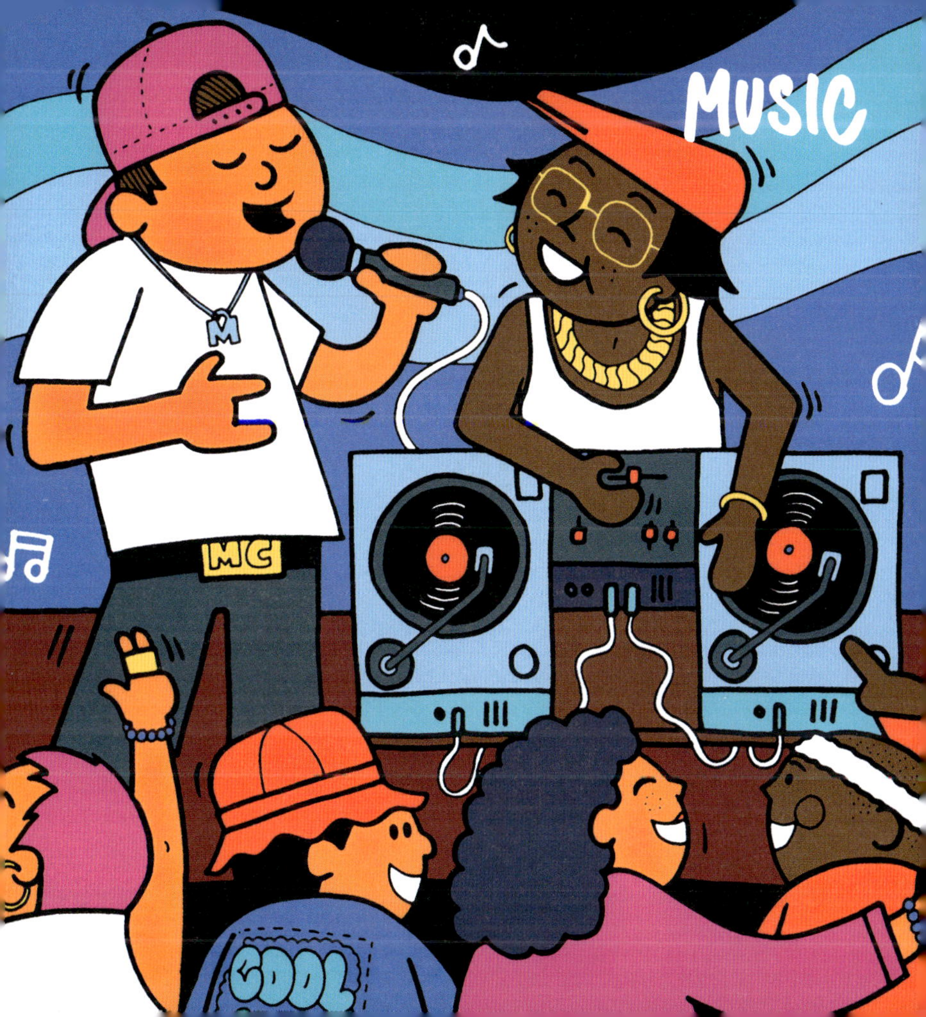
MUSIC
M
MC
COOL

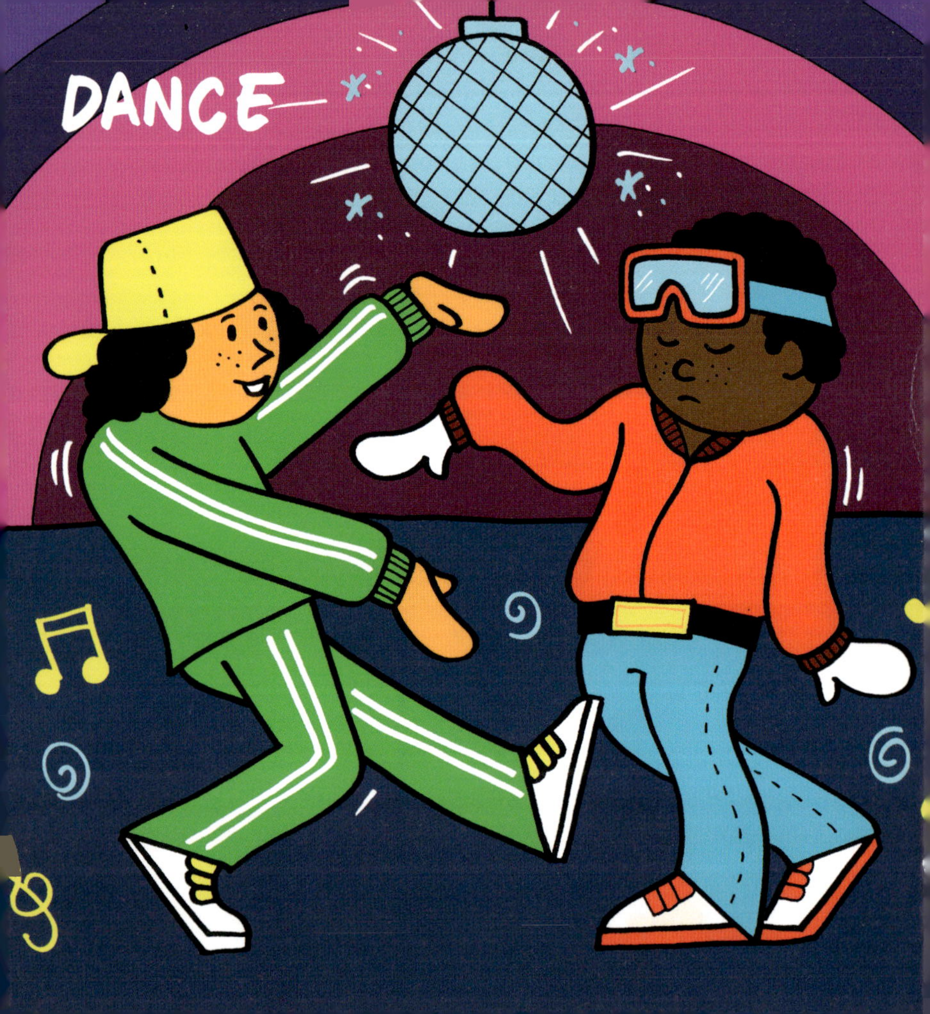
DANCE